GREAT BIBLE STORIES

THE STORY OF
ABRAHAM

Adapted by Maxine Nodel   Illustrated by Norman Nodel

BARONET BOOKS is a registered trademark of Playmore Inc., Publishers
and Waldman Publishing Corp., New York, N.Y.

Copyright © MCMXCIII Playmore Inc., Publishers
and Waldman Publishing Corp., New York, New York

All Rights Reserved.

BARONET BOOKS, NEW YORK, NEW YORK
Printed in China

Once there was a man named Abraham who lived in Haran, with his wife, Sarah. One day, God spoke with him.

"If you leave your country and people, and travel to a land I will show you, you will become the father of a great nation. I will bless your name and make it great."

So Abraham left his country and people and traveled to a new land where God had sent him.

The land of Canaan, where God had sent Abraham, was good to him, and Abraham grew rich in cattle, gold and silver.

One night, God spoke again to Abraham.

"Look up at the stars and count if you can. Your people will be as many as the stars in the sky."

Abraham looked sad.

"But I have no sons, and Sarah and I are too old to have children."

"You must have faith in me," God replied.

Soon after, in the heat of the day, Abraham, sitting in the shade of his tent, looked up suddenly to see three men standing before him.

Abraham sent for some water.

"Rest yourselves under a tree and I will get you some bread," he said.

Abraham rushed into the tent and said to Sarah, "Prepare some bread, cream, and milk."

Then Abraham set this food and some tender meat before the three men.

After they ate the three men said, "Abraham, your wife will
have a son and his name will be Isaac."
Sarah heard this and laughed.
"I am too old to have a baby," she said.

"Why does your wife laugh?" the men asked.
"Is there anything too difficult for the Lord to do?"

Abraham realized the men were sent by God,
and knew that he would have a son. Soon the three
strangers asked directions to two cities, Sodom and
Gomorra.

"There is much wickedness in these cities," the strangers said. "They must be destroyed."

Abraham was worried because his nephew, Lot, lived in the cities, so he pleaded with God.

"Will you spare these cities if you can find good men that live there?"

God said that he would save the cities if he could find ten good men that lived there. But the cities were so wicked that ten righteous people could not be found!

By this time, the three strangers had gone to Sodom and Gomorra. They warned Lot to flee before the cities were destroyed.

"Take your wife and daughters and run to the hills!"
they urged Lot.
    "Don't look back, for if you do, you will be destroyed!"
But Lot's wife did look back and was turned into a pillar of salt.

Soon the cities of Sodom and Gomorra were no more!

Months later, the stranger's promise came true.
Sarah and Abraham had a son.

Abraham and Sarah named their son Isaac, which means 'full of laughter' since Sarah had laughed by the tent when the strangers spoke.

Isaac grew up to be a wonderful son and Abraham and Sarah loved him very much.

Years later, when Isaac was still a young man, God put Abraham to a test.

God said, "Bring your son to the land of Moriah. There is a mountain there. Climb to the top. I would like you to sacrifice your son to me."

Because Abraham trusted God, he did as God asked him.
But deep inside he was sad, for he loved Isaac as much as a father
could love a son.

At the top of the mountain an Angel called out from heaven to Abraham:

"Abraham, Abraham, I know now how much you trust in God. You do not have to sacrifice your son."

Abraham and Isaac rejoiced and God blessed
them for their righteousness with a happy life
and many descendants.